DATE DUE

C.1

CC

DEMCO

SOCCER

SOCCER

The International Sport

Robert B. Jackson

Henry Z. Walck
A Division of
David McKay Company, Inc.
New York

ILLUSTRATION CREDITS
Jerry Liebman Studio, pages 10, 32, 33, 48, 52;
United Press International, pages 3, 7, 14, 19, 28, 35,
38, 40, 44 and 45, 50, 57.

Library of Congress Cataloging in Publication Data

Jackson, Robert B
Soccer: the international sport.

SUMMARY: Discusses the wide appeal of soccer, the international rules, amateur,
professional, and semi-professional teams, world cup finals, and the future of
soccer in the United States.
1. Soccer—Juvenile literature. [1. Soccer]
I. Title.
GV943.25.J33   796.33′4   78-54045
ISBN 0-8098-6450-9

10 9 8 7 6 5 4 3 2 1

Manufactured in the United States of America

Contents

1

"The Beautiful Game"

BRAZIL WAS ON THE ATTACK, and a midfielder boomed a long kick into the center of the field, just in front of the goal. The ball, aimed with pinpoint accuracy, dropped in the midst of four players.

Three were Swedish defenders, but the fourth was a young Brazilian forward. It was Pelé, then seventeen years old and playing in his first World Cup final.

While facing away from the goal, Pelé swiftly raised his right thigh to cushion the dropping ball. Then he bounced the ball from his thigh down to his right instep, and from there he kicked it gently back over his head. Avoiding the pressing defenders, he spun completely around toward the goal. Before the ball could reach the ground, Pelé kicked it again.

The Swedish goalkeeper flung himself headlong, arms outstretched. But he could not stop the ball from plunging between the goalpost and his fingertips into the net.

Brazil won the World Cup that year (1958), and Pelé was to become the greatest player in the history of soc-

Pelé (far right, arms raised) scores one of his two goals against Sweden in the 1958 World Cup final. He was then seventeen years old.

cer. But during that brief moment in front of the Swedish goal, he had done more than use great skill to score for his country. He had also given a remarkable demonstration of the astonishing control and grace that are part of what he calls "the beautiful game."

2

International Sport

MANY OF US IN THE UNITED STATES are dedicated sports fans. We spend much of our spare time playing, watching, and talking about sports. Nearly every school has a strong sports program. Big crowds flock to professional events. Sports programs get top television ratings. And millions have taken up at least one sport on a participatory basis.

But sports-minded as most of us are, we have not paid much attention to soccer until recently. We have neglected a sport that is played in nearly every other country in the world. Totals of membership in the United Nations and FIFA (the international soccer organization) are just now about equal.

Wherever soccer is played, it is usually the most popular sport by far. In fact, the passion for soccer in other countries is more intense than the enthusiasm for any U.S. sport. Monday Night Football, the World Series, and the Stanley Cup are taken very seriously here, but an important soccer game elsewhere produces even greater excitement.

Major soccer stadiums are, therefore, very large. The biggest stadium in the National Football League (the Los Angeles Memorial Coliseum) can hold 90,000 spectators, and the largest baseball park (the Cleveland Stadium) has a capacity of 76,713. In comparison, soccer stadiums with capacities of 100,000 are common in both Europe and South America. Biggest of them all is Maracaná Stadium in Rio de Janeiro, Brazil, which has held 200,000. To get some idea of what a typical Maracaná crowd is like, multiply an average World Series turnout by four and then equip most of the fans with whistles, trumpets, and firecrackers.

Soccer also attracts a vast television audience in other countries. The largest number of viewers for any televised sports event in the U.S. to date was the eighty-six million who watched the 1978 Super Bowl. But it was predicted that six hundred million soccer fans would watch the 1978 World Cup final on television.

Avid soccer followers in some countries are even willing to pay for closed circuit television broadcasts of the World Cup draw, during which no soccer at all is played. The draw is only a preliminary meeting at which qualifying teams are matched by chance for the opening round.

Soccer fans often get more emotional about their sport, too. Unfortunately, such deep feelings can sometimes cause serious trouble. In South America, for instance, many of the soccer fields have to be surrounded by ditches filled with water. These moats protect players and officials from excited spectators in the stands.

The new stadium in Buenos Aires, Argentina,
site of the 1978 World Cup final.

Recently in England, a First Division club had to be barred from playing Cup matches for three years because of fighting by its supporters. Much worse, soccer riots have caused both injuries and death. In 1964, during a riot in Lima, Peru, following an Olympic qualifying match, 300 people were killed and 500 were injured.

Another outburst from soccer fans was reputed to have caused a short war. Tension already existed between Honduras and El Salvador in 1969 when the two Central American countries played a World Cup match. Rioting broke out after the very close game, and diplomatic relations were then broken. El Salvador invaded Honduras, and the "Soccer War" that followed lasted for several days.

On the other hand, soccer has also been credited with stopping combat. On Christmas Day, 1914, during World War I, British and German soldiers on the Western Front are said to have played soccer together. Also, at the height of the Nigerian civil war in Africa, both sides are supposed to have made a temporary peace in order to watch Pelé play in an exhibition match.

3

The Fascination of Soccer

WHY DOES SOCCER have such a strong appeal for so many people? For one thing, soccer is simpler to follow than most other games, including football and baseball. Soccer is basically a matter of two teams moving continuously up and down a long field, each trying to put the ball into the other's net. There are few rules, no timeouts (except for major injuries), and no complex statistics to keep. Only a very small number of substitutions are allowed.

Another reason for the fascination of soccer is that its action is almost nonstop as compared to the stop-and-go pace of baseball and football. Soccer also has greater visibility; the ball is always in sight and the stands are often located at the very edge of the field or "pitch."

The lack of special equipment for the players increases interest for spectators as well. Players wear shirts, shorts, long socks, and low-cut shoes. Without such items as helmets to hide their faces, they are easily seen by the fans. Favorites are quickly recognized, and facial expressions during the game can be observed.

Soccer fans get to see more of the players' faces
than do football spectators. The strain and effort of competition are more visible.

Soccer fans identify more easily with the players in still another way. In contrast to basketball and football, soccer is played by people of average size, even at the top rank level. For example, Pelé is only five feet, nine inches tall, and weighs 165 pounds. A soccer player does not need to be unusually tall or burly. Instead it is skill, speed, imagination, and endurance that are required.

Soccer's basic rule is "Play the ball, not the person." This means that body contact, made by chance while playing the ball, is permitted. Such contact can be bone-jarring, of course, particularly without equipment. But while shoulder-to-shoulder charging is legal, the deliberate holding, pushing, tripping, and blocking of other contact sports are not allowed. Thus, the size of the player is not as important, and soccer is generally safer to play.

Because soccer players do not need to be built like giants or weight-lifters to be competitive, children and women, as well as men, enjoy playing the game. This wider participation has also helped to increase general interest in soccer as a spectator sport.

Most fans are aware of the great physical demands made upon soccer players. With the exception of the goalkeeper, soccer players must be in motion during almost all of a game. Under international rules, they play constantly throughout two forty-five–minute halves. The pace rarely slows, and there is never any chance to rest on a bench or relax in a dugout. One professional has said that he runs eight miles and loses twelve pounds in every game. Another commented that during an average match, he runs for eighty-five minutes to touch the ball for five.

Knowledgeable spectators also appreciate the fact that soccer is a game best played by a smoothly working team. A group playing merely to support one or two superstars will not be successful, because the sport demands that everyone play together unselfishly.

In addition, the fans realize that each player must think for himself or herself throughout a game. A few set plays can be practiced beforehand, but for the most part it is the players themselves who decide the course of each play on the spot. This constant improvisation is completely different from football, in which each play is worked out ahead of time by a staff of coaches, and often sent into the game by them at the proper time.

Still, when 100 thousand cheering soccer enthusiasts turn out for a big match, they probably don't think very much about these general advantages. What they applaud is crisp quick passing, deft footwork, and agile thrusting of the ball by the players' heads. They look for the dazzling kicks and runs that can instantly turn defense into offense. For the fans, the best part of soccer is the excitement of its continuous goal-to-goal action.

4

The Real Football

VARIOUS HISTORIANS have traced the beginnings of soccer back to ancient Rome or China, but the game as we know it originated in England. During the Middle Ages, entire English villages would play a form of soccer with hundreds of men on each side. They would swarm against each other, moving the ball back and forth between their two towns by any means possible. So many people got hurt in these scrambling brawls that several kings tried to ban them.

A more civilized form of the game was then developed during the eighteenth century at English schools and universities. The exact rules varied from school to school. Some schools allowed the ball to be moved with either the hands or the feet, while others permitted use of only the feet.

In 1863, the Football Association was formed in England to regulate the game that used only the feet. The other version, which allowed the handling of the ball, eventually developed into rugby, an ancestor of U.S. football.

Soccer is the favorite sport in South America and almost everywhere in the world. Here are Little League-type players in Brazil.

Football became firmly established in England, and was then exported around the world to grow into an international sport. British seamen, colonists, missionaries, and military men played the game wherever they went, particularly in Europe and South America.

One exception, of course, was the United States. The game was not only unpopular here, there was even a problem with its name. To this day, we disagree with the rest of the world on the name of the world's most played sport. What everyone else still calls football we refer to as soccer, our football being a different game.

The word "soccer" is probably British slang. The sport, regulated by the Football Association, came to be called Association Football, and "soc" is thought to be an abbreviation for association. "Cer" was added to "soc" because it was considered fashionable to talk this way in English schools. Rugby was often called "rugger," for example.

One explanation for soccer's being rejected in the United States for so long was that many people wanted to be independent of any European influence. Many Americans looked down on the sport because it came from another country, and thought of soccer as a game to be played only by immigrants.

Soccer was also dismissed by the major U.S. colleges in favor of rugby. What is usually referred to as the first intercollegiate football game in this country— between Princeton and Rutgers in 1869—was actually a form of soccer. But Harvard and Yale chose to play rugby instead, and other schools soon followed their example. Before long, soccer was abandoned by most schools and rugby was gradually transformed into our present-day football.

But, as we shall see, the United States is now starting to make up for lost time in a big way. U.S. sports fans are finally sharing in the enjoyment of soccer, both as players and spectators. The popularity of soccer is spreading rapidly in schools and colleges, and professional soccer is at last becoming an outstanding U.S. spectator sport.

5

On the Pitch

A SOCCER TEAM (or side) has eleven players. A goal-keeper is stationed at the mouth of the goal as the last line of defense, while the ten other players move freely and continuously all over the pitch. They either attack or defend as play develops.

The only way to score in soccer is to move the ball completely past the goal line. Most of the time, this will be the goal line of the opposing side. However, a team unfortunate enough to misplay a ball into its own goal will score an "own goal" for the other side.

The ball can be moved in several ways, but use of the hands is against the rules. And according to the anatomy of soccer, one's hands reach all the way up to the arm pits. Unless the ball happens to hit the hand accidentally, a "hand-ball" stops play and the other side takes over. The players say that "ball-to-hand" is allowed but "hand-to-ball" is not.

There are two exceptions to the "hands" rule. First, goalkeepers are permitted to use their hands to stop the ball, throw it back down the pitch, or roll it to another player. Second, if the ball goes off the pitch at either side, a "throw-in" is made. A member of the team that did *not* touch the ball last stands outside the pitch at its edge. He or she then throws the ball back into play with both hands from behind the head.

While the ball can be moved on the pitch with any part of the body other than the hands and arms, it is primarily the feet that are used to control the ball. A combination of kicking and running is often used in taking the ball away from the opposing team, in passing it from player to player, and in trying to score.

Next in importance to the feet is the head. Newcomers to soccer often find it most unusual that the ball is butted with the forehead for considerable distances. But many passes are made and many goals are scored in this way. Other parts of the body used to control the ball are the chest, thighs, and knees.

Soccer is a fluid and free-wheeling game in which a team switches quickly from offense to defense. Within seconds, a side may be attacking, then defending, and then attacking again. In the past, European teams were noted for their defensive play, and South American sides were famous for attacking. The current trend, however, is one toward "total soccer." This means that each player does his or her utmost at both offense and defense during an entire game.

Nevertheless, the eleven positions on a soccer side are usually divided into three groups. First is the defensive group, of which the most important member is the goalkeeper. The keeper is helped by three or four backs whose chief area of responsibility extends from the goal

"Heading" in soccer means pushing the ball with the forehead to pass or shoot. Several players often leap into the air at the same time, competing for the ball.

line to just past midfield. These defenders try to stop the other team's offense, and then return the ball downfield. Often a "sweeper," one who roams behind the other backs, has the duty of catching up with loose balls and opponents who break away from everyone else.

Most of the work of the attackers takes place on the other half of the pitch, where their chief purpose is to score. Of the usual three or four forwards, the two on the outside near the edges of the pitch are called "wings." They feed crossing passes to the central "strikers" and also shoot for goals themselves. Ideally, forwards are lightning fast runners and highly accurate shooters.

Linking the defenders to the attackers are two or three midfielders, also called halfbacks. They pass the ball from the defenders to the attackers, and play defense as well. Midfielders are usually the best passers on the side and the busiest people on the pitch.

The exact number of players within each of these three groups varies according to the style of each team and the strategy of each game. Such formations are usually described by numerical terms such as 4–3–3 or 4–2–4. The first figure gives the number of defensive players, not counting the goalkeeper. The second figure indicates the number of midfielders, and the third shows how many attackers there are. A 4–2–4 formation would thus emphasize offense more than a 4–3–3. The lineup for a kickoff is 2–3–5.

The system by which the players themselves are numbered on their shirts varies from country to country, but goalkeepers are always assigned number 1. Generally, low numbers are given to defenders, while higher numbers indicate attackers. In such cases, any number over 11 belongs to a substitute.

Players dress in colorful shirts, shorts, and long socks called "strips." Each team has its own official color scheme. The goalkeeper wears a shirt of a different color so as to be instantly recognized. (One famous keeper for Dynamo of Moscow, who dressed all in black, was known as "The Black Octopus.") A goalkeeper is allowed to wear gloves for a better grip in bad weather, and a cap to shade the eyes from the sun, if needed.

International rules do not require that shoes be worn, but nearly all players regard them as their most important piece of equipment. Rules limit the length of any studs or cleats, according to weather conditions. Should players desire, they can also wear shin guards under their socks.

The ball they use is twenty-seven inches in diameter, a bit smaller and lighter than a basketball. Most are white for visibility, and some have additional colored spots to help players judge the ball's rotation.

Soccer pitches are not as uniform in size as U.S. football fields, but under international rules they are almost always larger. The ideal size is recommended to be 115 yards long and 75 yards wide. (U.S. football fields have a playing area 100 yards long and 53⅓ yards wide.) In the United States, official college pitches range from 110 to 120 yards in length, and from 65 to 75 yards in width. High-school pitches are allowed the same widths, and can vary from 100 to 120 yards in length.

As in football, the end-markings of a pitch are called goal lines. What would be the sidelines in football are

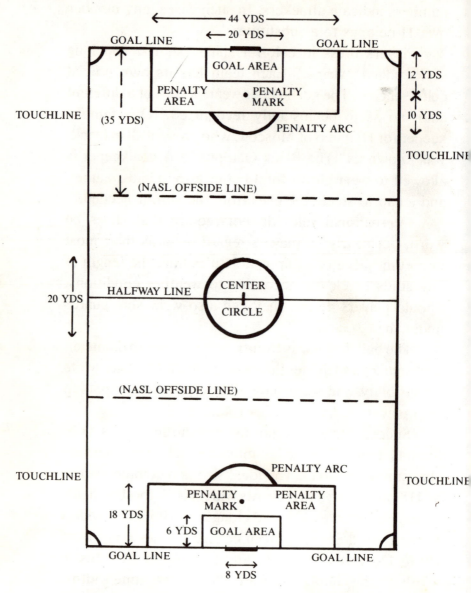

A soccer pitch can be anywhere from 50 to 100 yards wide, and 100 to 130 yards long, according to international rules.

called "touchlines" in soccer. Unlike a football field, a soccer pitch has no yard lines, but there is a "halfway line," which crosses the pitch at midfield and corresponds to football's fifty-yard line.

The kickoff by the forwards at the start of each half and after each goal is made from the center of the halfway line. A circle with a ten-yard radius is laid out around this point, and no opposing team member can enter this center circle until the ball is in play.

Two eight-feet-high goalposts are set into the ground twenty-four feet apart on each goal line. A crossbar connects the goalposts at the top, and the opening is usually backed with nets to make it easier to tell when a goal has been scored.

Two areas are outlined on the pitch in front of each goal. The "goal area" is twenty yards wide and six yards deep. If an attacking team puts the ball out of play over the goal line (without scoring, of course), the defending team is allowed to kick the ball downfield from within this goal area.

The goal area is part of a larger rectangle, the "penalty area." Forty-four yards wide and eighteen yards deep, this area is the most important part of the pitch. An attacker who is fouled within the "box" gets a chance for a penalty kick toward the goal. As the kick is made, all defending players must remain outside the penalty area, and only the goalkeeper is left to try to prevent a very likely goal. The two spots where penalty kicks are taken are marked on the pitch, twelve yards out from each goal line. Incidentally, when goalkeepers venture outside the penalty area, they can no longer touch the ball with their hands.

A soccer match is controlled by three officials. The referee, who runs along with play on the pitch, has absolute authority to interpret the rules and make all decisions. The referee is assisted by two linesmen who follow the play, one along each touchline. The linesmen carry flags with which they signal when the ball goes out of play and when certain rules are broken.

6

Kicks and Cautions

SOCCER IS A SIMPLE, straightforward game, but one rule can be confusing. This is the offside rule, similar to the offside rule of hockey, although not as complicated.

The purpose of the offside rule is to prevent a player from remaining near the goal, taking a long pass from downfield, and then scoring an easy goal at short range. While such a play is legal in basketball where it is called a "cripple shot", it is not allowed in soccer.

The offside rule states that attacking players cannot run ahead of the ball unless there are at least two defenders (three, by women's rules) between them and the goal line, at the time the ball is played. One of these defenders can be the goalkeeper.

The offside rules does *not* apply, however, if the ball was last touched by an opponent, such as a clearing pass from the goalkeeper. Players cannot be called offside within their own half of the pitch, either.

The linesmen signal offside to the referee from the touchlines by raising their flags in the air, and the referee then decides whether to stop play for a penalty. Offside is often a difficult judgment to make because of the speed at which players change positions. The rule is not invoked against those players who may be technically offside for a moment but are not involved in the play at the time.

Indirect Free Kick

The penalty for being offside is an indirect free kick, awarded to the defending team. Play is halted, and the ball is placed at the spot where the offside occurred. The penalized team must remain ten yards away from the ball, while any member of the opposing team takes an indirect free kick. "Indirect" means that a goal cannot be scored directly from such a kick; another player must touch the ball first.

Indirect free kicks are also awarded for five other reasons. These infractions include intentionally blocking an opponent when not playing the ball, and charging into an opponent when the ball is not within playing distance. Others are dangerous play, such as high-kicking near an opponent, and charging into a goalkeeper who does not have the ball. And the goalkeeper can give up an indirect free kick by taking more than four steps before throwing, kicking, or bouncing the ball.

The referee signals an indirect free kick by blowing a whistle and by raising an arm in the air until the kick has been taken.

Direct Free Kick

Direct free kicks are awarded to the opposing side for nine types of more serious misplay. A direct free kick is taken in the same way as an indirect free kick, but a goal may be scored directly without any other player touching the ball.

A direct free kick is taken after an opposing player has tripped, kicked, or pushed. Hitting, holding, and jumping at a player are also offenses penalized by a direct free kick, as are charging dangerously, charging from behind, and playing the ball with hands or arms. The referee signals a direct free kick by blowing the whistle and pointing.

Penalty Kick

Direct free kicks are not awarded within the penalty area. When one of the nine types of fouls—causing a direct free kick elsewhere on the pitch—takes place in the penalty area, a penalty kick is given instead.

Before a penalty kick is made, all but the goalkeeper and the player taking the penalty kick must leave the penalty area. Other players are required to remain ten yards away from the ball, which is placed on the penalty mark twelve yards straight back from the center of the goal line. The arc of the circle joining the penalty box defines the ten-yard limit. The goalkeeper cannot move his or her feet until the ball has been kicked.

The one-on-one competition between a goalkeeper and a penalty kicker trying to outguess each other is much like that of a penalty shot in hockey. However, a soccer goal is much larger than a hockey goal, and therefore far more difficult to defend. "Saves" are not nearly as frequent.

Cautions

The referee has the power to "caution" a player for such misconduct as "unsportsmanlike play" and for dis-

A keeper about to "let in" a World Cup goal from a penalty kick. He is moving in the wrong direction.

agreeing with official decisions. A referee can also eject a player from a game for a very serious foul or for violent behavior. No replacement is then allowed.

A caution is generally indicated by the referee's showing the player a yellow card. At that time, the referee also writes the player's name in a little book. Once a player has thus been "booked," any further serious misconduct will bring expulsion. (Team officials can also be cautioned for such offenses as coaching from the touchlines.)

A player is expelled, or "sent off," by being shown a red card. In many of the instances requiring caution or expulsion, a free kick is awarded, too.

In certain foul situations, the referee will apply the "advantage rule." If the team that has been fouled still appears to retain an advantage—say a tripping effort has failed and the fouled player is about to shoot anyway—the referee will not call the foul so that play can continue.

Goal Kick

To be out of bounds in soccer, the ball must be *completely* across the touchline or goal line. A ball that has any part still touching the line is in play, and the location of the person playing that ball makes no difference. A kicker may be outside the line and the ball on the line, still in play.

If the attacking team puts the ball out of play over the goal line, the defending team is awarded a goal kick. A goal kick is taken from within that half of the goal area nearer to where the ball crossed the goal line. A goal kick must clear the penalty area, and is usually made by the keeper. Opponents are not allowed in the penalty area when a goal kick is being made.

Corner Kick

When it is the defending team that sends the ball out of play over the goal line, the attackers are given a corner kick. Corner kicks are taken from within that marking at the corner of the pitch closest to where the ball went out. Opponents must stay at least ten yards away from the ball until the kick has been made.

Corner kicks are highly dangerous plays against which to defend. The ball is usually crossed directly into the goal area, where one quick header can score. Therefore, teams practice set plays in advance, both making and defending against corner kicks. Corner kicks and goal kicks are signaled by the linesmen, who point flags in the attacking direction of the team entitled to the ball. As always, final approval is up to the referee.

Throw-In

When the ball goes completely outside either touchline, the linesman on that side points a flag to indicate the team that is to get the ball. As in basketball, it is the team that did *not* touch the ball last. A member of this team—usually a midfielder—then throws the ball into play from the point at which it went out. Unlike a basketball throw-in, a soccer throw-in must be made from behind the head with both hands. A strong throw-in can carry forty yards and can often be as much of a threat as a corner kick.

The offside rule does not apply to goal kicks, corner kicks, or throw-ins.

7

Soccer Skills

Dribbling

IN SOCCER, dribbling does not mean bouncing the ball
with one hand while running, as it does in basketball.
Soccer players dribble by advancing the ball with short
kicks as they run along behind it. As in basketball, the
aim is to keep the ball under complete control at all times.

Skilled dribblers can speed past or around defenders. They can bring the ball to a complete stop in a
twinkling and then change direction, or they may even
flick the ball between defenders' legs. Dribblers also try
to trick the opposition if they can. They may feint in one
direction, forcing the defender to move that same way,
then dart away on another course and leave the defender
behind.

Tackling

When a soccer player dribbles, the opposition tries
to take the ball away by tackling. Tackling may not mean
what you expect, either, for it is much different from

Soccer players "dribble" by advancing the ball
with short kicks as they run along behind it.

An opposing player tries to take the ball away
from a dribbler by "tackling."

football tackling. Under soccer rules, tacklers can use only their feet.

Often a pursuing tackler is able to steal the ball from a dribbler with a mere tap of the foot. But at other times, a tackler must slide feetfirst, like a baseball player, into a dribbler. In any case, tacklers must be careful to avoid being penalized for tripping or kicking.

Kicking

Soccer kicks range from a short pass off the knee, to a clearing punt by the goalkeeper, to a whistling "banana shot" that curves into the net for a goal. Twenty different types of kicks are possible in soccer, but surprising to most American fans, the ball is seldom kicked with the toe. Most soccer kicks are made with the instep, the outside of the foot, the inside of the foot, the sole, or even backward from the heel.

Good soccer kickers can blast low drives, lift high lobs, and boom swerving balls that are hard to defend against. They can kick backward as well as frontward, to either side, from midair, and from the ground. (Kicking while the ball is still in the air is called volleying.) The best players also kick equally well with both feet, and look down on someone who "has only one foot."

The most spectacular kick of all is the overhead, or bicycle kick. The kicker faces the oncoming ball and leaps into the air so as to be parallel with the ground, facing upward. During the fraction of a second that the kicker can remain in this position, the ball is kicked over the head with a bicycling motion.

Although fans loudly cheer the dramatic aspects of a

The overhead, or bicycle, kick is one of soccer's most spectacular plays.

bicycle kick, the most important elements of kicking are speed and accuracy. A pass or shot must reach exactly the right spot at the right time, otherwise an opposing player will get the ball. Long kicks are usually avoided because they can be blown by the wind and because they give the defense more time to adjust while the ball is in the air.

Trapping

A moving ball must often be brought under control before it can be dribbled, passed, or shot. Trapping is a gentle, cushioning action that uses the head, chest, thighs, or feet to drop the ball at the player's feet. If done awkwardly, the ball will bounce out of control, perhaps into possession of the opposition.

Heading

Heading is another basic method of passing and scoring. One of the biggest thrills for spectators is the sight of two competing players springing high in the air, and the attacker being able to head the ball into the net.

Heading is done with the forehead so that the player can watch the ball continuously. Coaches, therefore, advise players to "throw the eyes" at an approaching ball. As with soccer's other techniques, accurate heading requires a great deal of practice, sometimes with a ball hanging at the end of a rope.

Much practice and thought are also needed to blend all these skills into well-played soccer. Suppose we examine an imaginary match for a time and see how the skills are combined on the pitch.

The Magpies' goalkeeper clears his goal with a thumping punt out to one of his midfielders. The midfielder chests the ball down to the ground and kicks a quick pass further downfield, just in front of a swiftly running Magpie forward.

Before the forward can catch up, a Canary defender kicks the ball back upfield. A Canary midfielder traps the ball with his foot near the touchline and begins to dribble toward the Magpie goal.

Starting left and running right, he weaves past two Magpie defenders and dodges down the side of the pitch. Closely marked (guarded) by still another defender, he screens the ball with his body and flicks it along the ground to an advancing Canary forward.

As the Canary forward dribbles rapidly toward the goal, a Magpie back attempts a sliding tackle. The forward chips a short pass over the would-be tackler to a teammate, keeps running at top speed, and takes the ball back again on a return pass.

This type of play is known as a "give-and-go" in basketball, but is called a "wall pass" in soccer. The name comes from the fact that young players often practice it in the street by kicking the ball against a wall and playing the rebound. (The wall pass is not the same thing as "the wall." The wall is formed for defensive purposes against free kicks by several players who stand side by side with linked arms.)

The Canary forward lofts a crossing kick into the penalty box, where one of his strikers is able to leap higher than a colliding defender. He heads the ball directly at the goal, aiming inside the nearer post just below the crossbar.

37

A leaping save by an agile goalkeeper.

Goalkeepers keep their bodies behind approaching balls if they can, catching shots with both hands and pulling them in close. The worst thing that can happen to a keeper, other than letting in a goal, is to have the ball rebound into play again and give the attackers a second chance. Only when there is no other choice will a keeper dive for the ball, try to punch it away, or attempt to tip it backward over the crossbar. And even if a keeper can put a ball out of play without a goal in one of these ways, according to the rules, the attackers then get a corner kick. A "corner" is to be avoided, if possible, because it can set up a goal in itself.

In this case, however, the Magpie goalkeeper was helped temporarily by the post, the traditional "best friend" of all keepers. But when the hard shot struck the post, the ball glanced off to an unmarked Canary nearby. He promptly drilled it into the net, and as the rest of his team crushed around him in happy triumph, he punched both arms into the air.

Most countries in Europe and South America have their own professional soccer leagues. The English league has a notable tradition, but many think the best soccer is currently being played in the West German league. In this German match, the prone keeper has failed to smother a goal.

8

The World of Soccer

THE SPORT OF SOCCER is controlled throughout the world by the *Fédération Internationale de Football Association,* or FIFA. Over 140 countries belong to FIFA, and its headquarters are in Zurich, Switzerland. The membership is made up of representatives from national soccer associations of each country, such as the United States Soccer Federation.

FIFA registers individual players of three types: amateur, professional, and semiprofessional. The majority are amateur, and at one time their strongest competition was found at the Olympics.

Unfortunately, in recent years Olympic soccer has been weakened by the same problem that has plagued much of international amateur sport. The Eastern Communist countries do not distinguish between amateur and professional athletes; athletes who would be classified as professionals elsewhere are regarded as amateurs in Eastern Europe.

Since the Western countries do not allow professionals to play in the same games as amateurs, their teams are at a disadvantage when they play Eastern teams. Because of this difference, no Western entry has won the Olympic soccer tournament since 1948.

The best soccer in the West is played in the professional leagues. Nearly every country in Europe, Central America, and South America has its own league, and spectator interest is much stronger than in any U.S. sport. As a result, there are many more teams relative to the size of the population than could be supported by any one sport in this country. For instance, the First Division alone of the English Football League has twenty-two teams, and there are four divisions in all.

The divisions of U.S. professional leagues are usually set up on a geographical basis, but the divisions of European soccer leagues are decided by level of play. The best teams are in the First Division, and the least successful teams play in the lowest division. Teams from different divisions do not meet in league play. In our terms, the First Division is "big league," while the other divisions are supporting "minors."

Another big difference from U.S. sports organization is that league soccer teams can move from division to division. At the end of each season, the two or three teams in each division with the worst records are dropped to the next lower division. This is called relegation. A comparable situation would be if the New York Knicks finished last in the National Basketball Association and then had to play the next year in the Eastern Basketball Association, along with Quincy, Massachusetts, and Asbury Park, New Jersey.

The opposite of soccer relegation is promotion. The

leading two or three teams of each division move up the next year to play in the next higher division. There can be no promotion from the First Division, of course, and its winner is the league champion. The league champions of each country in Europe meet the following season in an elimination tournament. That winning team receives the European Cup.

In most European countries, league teams also play a second series of games during their regular season. This is Cup competition, in which teams from all divisions play each other once. Losers are eliminated, and the final winner takes the Cup. Generally, Cup winners come from the First Division, but this is not always so. All the Cup winners of European countries then compete to determine which club will be awarded the European Cup Winners' Cup.

In South America, an annual competition similar to the European Cup is held, and the winner receives the *Copa Libertadores* (Liberator's Cup). The European Cup winner then plays the *Copa Libertadores* winner for the World Club Championship.

Over the years, there have been league teams and players who have become world-famous. One such team is *Real Madrid* of Spain, which dominated European soccer during the 1950s. (*Real* means royal, the team having been given that title by a Spanish king.) *Real Madrid* won the European Cup five times in a row between 1956 and 1960, again in 1966, and the World Club Championship in 1960.

Like many other professional European clubs, *Real Madrid* recruits its players from all over the world, not

Eusebio, the great Portuguese star, has a shot stopped by the famous Russian keeper, "Black Octopus" Lev Yashin.

just from within its own borders. Stars on *Real Madrid* have come from Hungary, France, Uruguay, and other countries. One of the greatest stars was an Argentinian, Alfredo di Stefano. A center forward, he was called the "White Arrow" because his bald head showed up so clearly on the pitch.

U.S. professional teams often exchange players by trading them, but soccer clubs generally buy players directly from each other for a transfer fee. One of the biggest transfer fees to date exceeded two million dollars, a large amount by the standards of any professional sport. *Barcelona, Real Madrids's* biggest rival, paid *Ajax* of Amsterdam that sum for forward Johan Cruyff. The slender superstar had led *Ajax* to three straight European Cup Championships from 1971 to 1973, and many thought he would become the next Pelé.

Benfica of Lisbon, Portugal, was a very strong team during the 1960s, primarily because of the attacking play of the "Black Panther," Eusebio. A fabled shooter, Eusebio Ferreira da Silva grew up in poverty in Mozambique and learned his kicking skills while barefoot. He averaged more than forty goals a season in Europe and once made thirty-nine penalty shots in a row.

Because organized soccer originated in England, many of the present English clubs have long histories. Such clubs as Arsenal (started by London munitions workers and referred to as the "Gunners"), Tottenham Hotspur (the "Spurs" of London), and Manchester United (the "Red Devils") have fielded outstanding sides.

Of the many celebrated English players, fans still

talk about such stars as defensive ace Bobby Moore, and Bobby Charlton, the balding midfielder. Most remembered of all, though, is Sir Stanley Matthews, who was made a knight for his soccer accomplishments. A short, slight winger, he became a professional at the age of seventeen, and still played First Division matches at the age of fifty. Matthews was one of the most skilled dribblers of all time, and never received a caution from a referee throughout his long career.

At present, English soccer has declined somewhat, and the best soccer in Europe is being played by West Germany. In the past Italian teams, such as *Internazionale* and *Milan*, have also been dominant. The Italian clubs were known for their defensive play and the great wealth that allowed them to sign many of the best players.

But while national soccer fortunes often rise and fall with the times, many local rivalries remain constantly intense. One of the most heated is between Glasgow Celtic and Glasgow Rangers of the Scottish League; in the English League, Everton and Liverpool (both from Liverpool) are another pair of traditional rivals.

There are many strong soccer clubs in Central and South America, too. *Peñarol* of Uruguay is a good example. Originally founded in 1891 under British influence to play cricket, *Peñarol* has been national champion of Uruguay year after year and World Club Champion in 1961 and 1966.

Most famous of all American teams is *Santos* of Brazil. *Santos* has made several world tours to play exhibition games, which are called "friendlies" in soccer.

Pelé, soccer's biggest star, played for both *Santos* of Brazil and the Cosmos of the North American Soccer League.

But *Santos* is even better known for having been the team of Pelé, soccer's biggest star.

Pelé, whose real name is Edson Arantes do Nacimento, was able to control the ball better than anyone else, and he was probably the most accurate passer and shooter as well. Pelé could also improvise brilliant scoring plays, one after another. His dignity, unassuming personality, and gentle smile made him highly popular with the fans.

Besides individual clubs organized into leagues, most soccer-playing countries also have national teams. The players on the national teams are selected from among the league clubs, much as U.S. "All-Star" teams are picked. Coaches of the national teams may be from any country, but players must be citizens of the selecting country. Thus, Franz Beckenbauer, who plays regularly for the Cosmos in the United States, would have been a member of the German national team for World Cup competition if the Cosmos had been willing to release him.

Players chosen for a national team are said to have been "capped." (In England they still receive honorary velvet caps with long tassels.) The number of caps a player is reported to have indicates the the number of times he has played on a national team. (A "cap" should not be confused with the "hat trick," a considerable feat in which one player scores three goals during a single game.)

National teams in Europe compete for the European Football Championship; South American national teams play for the South American Football Championship.

This goal against the Netherlands won the World Cup for West Germany in 1974.

But the most important event for all national teams is the World Cup.

The World Cup is the supreme event of soccer. It is a true international event with all countries eligible to compete, unlike the World Series of baseball, which is open to only two countries. The World Cup is also the most closely followed of any sports event in the world.

World Cup finals take place every four years, alternating between sites in Europe and South America. The 1974 World Cup was played in Munich, Germany; and the 1978 World Cup was held in Buenos Aires and four other cities in Argentina. The 1982 World Cup will be decided in Madrid, Spain.

World Cup play is so involved that it starts almost two years before the finals occur. A lengthy, world-wide tournament must be conducted to reduce the many entries to a final fourteen. These fourteen, plus the defending champion and the team of the host country, then compete in an elimination event to determine the world champion. In 1978, the sixteen final qualifiers from over one hundred original entries were Argentina, Austria, Brazil, France, Hungary, Iran, Italy, Mexico, the Netherlands, Peru, Poland, Scotland, Spain, Sweden, Tunisia, and West Germany.

The most successful country in World Cup play, so far, has been Brazil, which has won three times. Uruguay, Italy, and West Germany have each won twice, and England once. Although Brazil and West Germany were considered equal favorites for the 1978 World Cup, Argentina was the winner.

Attendance at North American Soccer League games increases each year. Above is recent action between the Chicago Sting and the Cosmos.

9

Making Up for Lost Time

AS MIGHT BE EXPECTED, the United States has not done very well in World Cup competition over the years. But they got as far as the semifinals at the first World Cup meeting of 1930, and the surprising U.S. team of 1950 made soccer history.

England was making her first appearance in World Cup play that year, and the typically powerful English side was a big favorite to win. When England played the United States, the English coach kept such stars as Stanley Matthews on the bench. He rested them for later games because he regarded the U.S. side as being almost a joke. Nevertheless, in one of the most stunning upsets in the history of sport, the underdog U.S. side defeated England 1–0.

More true to form, however, the U.S. team was beaten by Chile in its next match; and since that one brief moment of glory in 1950, U.S. World Cup entries have been eliminated at an early stage. Realistically, it is likely to be some time before the U.S. can qualify for the World Cup again, much less think about winning it.

But U.S. fans are hoping that the recent soccer explosion among young people in this country will produce improved players who can win the World Cup eventually. Soccer is now growing faster than any other college sport, and almost a million boys and girls played in U.S. youth leagues during 1977.

While most of these players love the game for itself, financially pressed school officials find soccer attractive for another reason: two entire soccer teams can be outfitted for what it costs to equip only one football player.

Admittedly, soccer as played in some U.S. colleges at present retains considerable foreign influence. This was very apparent when Hartwick College, in Oneonta, New York, defeated the University of San Francisco for the National Collegiate Athletic Association title in 1977. Most of Hartwick's stars were British, and the San Francisco roster included players from Colombia, England, Ethiopia, Greece, Liberia, Nigeria, and Norway.

At the professional level, the North American Soccer League has also begun to thrive in the United States. This was not true in the league's early days, for the NASL originally got off to a very bad start. Formed in 1968 from two unsuccessful leagues that had been set up only one year before, the NASL was in serious trouble within the next year. Attendance was sparse and the faltering league shrunk from seventeen to only five teams.

Still, the once dying NASL has not only recovered, it has now expanded to a total of twenty-four clubs in two conferences. Older teams, such as the Dallas Tornados,

Cosmos, and Rochester Lancers, have recently been joined by several new clubs, including New England T ι Men, Detroit Express, and Colorado Caribous.

NASL teams play lengthy schedules from April through July, with play-offs in August and a NASL championship Soccer Bowl at the end of the season. NASL crowds have multiplied to the point that a new record for soccer attendance in this country—77,691—was set in 1977.

One of the biggest reasons for this sudden upsurge was the signing of the famed Pelé by the New York Cosmos. Pelé had already retired from *Santos* of Brazil by then, but came out of retirement to play for The Cosmos from 1975 to 1977. He led the Cosmos to the league championship in 1977, and then played his final farewell game in New York that fall. The match was between Cosmos and *Santos*, with Pelé playing the first half for Cosmos and the second for his old team. (Cosmos won, 2–1, and Pelé scored one of their goals.) As usual, he packed the stands, but his many public appearances off the pitch have made thousands of new friends for NASL soccer, too.

NASL clubs can have only a specified maximum number of foreign players on their rosters at any one time, and they can put only a limited number of foreign players on the pitch at once. In future seasons, these maximums are scheduled to get progressively smaller in order to favor U.S. players. Meanwhile, however, most of the best players are still being imported.

At first, the majority of the players from abroad were apt to be either of average ability or past their prime.

Their situation was similar to that of baseball's ex–big-leaguers who leave the U.S. to play in Japan,or the pro basketball players who are cut in this country and then compete in European leagues.

Eusebio played for Toronto and Las Vegas; and Gordon Banks, of England, once the greatest goalkeeper in the world, made a comeback with the Miami Toros. George Best, a controversial Irish midfielder who had never lived up to his enormous promise in England, was signed by Los Angeles. And, of course, there was Pelé, who received seven million dollars for being soccer's unofficial missionary to the U.S.

But recently, the NASL became important enough to attract players of world rank at the peak of their careers. The Cosmos alone acquired high-scoring forward Giorgio Chinaglia from *Lazio* of Italy; West German superstar Franz Beckenbauer from *Bayern Munich;* mid-fielder Vladislav Bogicevic, the former captain of Red Star of Yugoslavia; and Dennis Tueart, a First Division forward from Manchester City in England. As a result, the level of NASL play can only improve further, and could eventually equal that of the world's best professional leagues.

Two differences in the rules remain, though. The NASL feels that the low scores common in European soccer would not be popular here, so it has changed the offside rule in the hope of providing more scoring. Blue lines have been added across NASL pitches, thirty-five yards out from the goal lines. The offside rule is then applied only in those areas between the blue lines and the goal lines.

West German Franz Beckenbauer (left), a former Captain of the World Cup championship team and twice European Player of the Year, now plays for the NASL Cosmos.

The NASL also awards the points that determine league standings differently, again to emphasize scoring. Under the usual rules, two points are given for a win, one point for a tie, and none for a loss. In the NASL, a winning team gets six points, plus one extra point for each goal up to a maximum of three extra points. A losing team also gets one point for each goal scored, up to a maximum of three points.

The NASL gives no points for ties because they are not allowed to stand. Should a NASL game end in a tie, a "shootout" takes place. One or two seven-and-one-half-minute "sudden-death" overtime periods are played, and the first team to score wins. If no one scores within the fifteen minutes, each team then selects five players who alternately take penalty kicks. And if the score remains tied after all that, penalty shots are continued until another goal is scored.

Some soccer purists and players object to these changes by the NASL. But they can only approve of soccer's zooming importance as a sport in the United States. Thanks to the NASL plus the growing popularity of soccer among young players, the future of the sport in this country looks very bright indeed. The rest of the world is still wondering what took us so long.

contents

British & North American Readers:
Please note that Australian cup and
spoon measurements are metric. A quick
conversion guide appears on page 63.
A glossary explaining unfamiliar terms
and ingredients begins on page 60.

2 baked potatoes

Wash and scrub 4 large (1.2kg) potatoes; pierce each potato with fork. Place on oven tray; bake in hot oven about 1 hour or until tender. Or microwave on **HIGH (100%)** about 8 minutes, or until tender.

ham, corn and coleslaw filling

Combine 1 cup (80g) shredded cabbage with 1 medium (120g) coarsely grated carrot, 1/4 cup (60ml) mayonnaise and 2 teaspoons Dijon mustard in medium bowl. Cut tops from 4 baked potatoes; scoop out centres into medium bowl. Crush potato flesh; add 100g shredded ham and 130g can creamed corn; mix well. Fill potato shells with mixture; top with coleslaw.

crispy bacon, french onion and chive filling

Cut 4 bacon rashers into small pieces; cook in heated small non-stick pan until crisp. Cut tops from 4 baked potatoes; scoop out centres into medium bowl. Crush potato flesh; add 250g tub French Onion Dip, 1 tablespoon chopped fresh chives, 1 tablespoon olive oil, 1 teaspoon white wine vinegar and 1 clove crushed garlic; mix well. Fill potato shells with mixture.

roasted capsicum, spinach and ricotta filling

Quarter 1 medium (200g) red capsicum; remove seeds and membranes. Roast under grill or in very hot oven, skin-side up, until skin blisters and blackens. Wrap capsicum pieces in plastic or paper for 5 minutes, peel away skin; finely chop. Boil, steam or microwave 150g baby spinach leaves until tender; drain. Squeeze out excess water, chop roughly. Cut tops from 4 baked potatoes, scoop out centres into medium bowl. Crush potato flesh; add spinach, capsicum, 250g ricotta, 2 teaspoons chopped fresh dill, 2 chopped green onions and 1 tablespoon lemon juice in medium bowl; mix well. Fill potato shells with mixture.

roasted garlic, artichoke and basil filling

Place 1 bulb (70g) garlic onto oven tray, spray with cooking-oil spray; cook, uncovered, in moderately hot oven about 30 minutes or until garlic is soft. Cut bulb in half horizontally; squeeze garlic pulp into medium bowl. Cut tops from 4 baked potatoes scoop out centres into bowl. Crush potato flesh; add garlic, 400g can drained artichokes and 2 tablespoons olive oil; mix well. Stir in 1 tablespoon chopped fresh basil leaves; fill potato shells with mixture.

from left: roasted garlic, artichoke and basil filling; roasted capsicum, spinach and ricotta filling; crispy bacon, french onion and chive filling; ham, corn and coleslaw filling

Each topping makes enough for 4 pitta pocket breads.

4 pitta pocket breads

eggplant and cheese topping

1 tablespoon olive oil

1 medium (200g) green capsicum, sliced

2 cloves garlic, crushed

1 medium (150g) onion, sliced

4 (240g) baby eggplants, sliced

1/3 cup (80ml) tomato paste

200g goat cheese, crumbled

cabanossi and olive topping

1/3 cup (80ml) tomato paste

2 tablespoons chopped fresh basil leaves

2 sticks cabanossi, sliced

1/2 cup (60g) seeded black olives, halved

1 cup (100g) grated mozzarella cheese

bacon and artichoke topping

4 bacon rashers, chopped

1/3 cup (80ml) tomato paste

1/3 cup (50g) sun-dried tomatoes in oil, drained, chopped

8 canned artichoke hearts, drained, sliced

1 cup (100g) grated mozzarella cheese

Spread pocket breads with the topping of your choice, place pizzas on oven tray. Bake in moderately hot oven 15 minutes or until heated through and browned lightly.

Eggplant and Cheese Topping Heat oil in medium pan, add capsicum, garlic, onion and eggplant; cook, stirring until vegetables are just tender. Spread pocket breads with paste; top with eggplant mixture, sprinkle with cheese.

Cabanossi and Olive Topping Spread pocket breads with paste; sprinkle with basil, cabanossi, olives and cheese.

Bacon and Artichoke Topping Place bacon in medium pan, cook, stirring, until bacon is crisp, drain on absorbent paper. Spread pocket breads with paste; sprinkle with bacon, tomatoes, artichokes and cheese.

6 zucchini
slice

2 teaspoons olive oil

1 large (200g) onion, chopped finely

4 medium (480g) zucchini, grated coarsely

3 bacon rashers, chopped finely

1 cup (125g) grated cheddar cheese

³/₄ cup (110g) self-raising flour

¹/₂ cup (125ml) vegetable oil

4 eggs, beaten lightly

Oil 19cm x 29cm rectangular slice pan.
Heat oil in small pan; cook onion, stirring, until soft. Combine onion with remaining ingredients in medium bowl; mix well. Spread mixture into prepared pan; bake in moderate oven 35 minutes or until firm.

smoked salmon

and spinach pizzas

7

4 pitta pocket breads

$^1/_2$ cup (125ml) tomato pasta sauce

1 cup (125g) grated cheddar cheese

10 spinach leaves, shredded

100g smoked salmon pieces

1 small (80g) onion, sliced

2 teaspoons drained capers

1 cup (125g) grated cheddar cheese, extra

$^1/_2$ teaspoon dried dill

$^1/_4$ cup (60ml) sour cream

Spread pocket breads with sauce; top with cheese, spinach, salmon, onion and capers, sprinkle with extra cheese and dill. Place pizzas on oven tray, bake in moderately hot oven about 15 minutes or until heated through. Top with dollops of sour cream, return to oven for 1 minute or until cream is warm.

8

chicken and basil

pizza

2¹/₃ cups (600ml) bottled tomato pasta sauce

1 long loaf Turkish pide

¹/₂ cup firmly packed fresh basil leaves

2 cups (300g) cooked chicken, shredded

200g fetta cheese, crumbled

¹/₂ cup (40g) coarsely grated parmesan cheese

¹/₂ cup (50g) coarsely grated mozzarella cheese

Pour sauce into medium pan. Bring to boil; simmer, uncovered, about 5 minutes or until thickened slightly.

Meanwhile, halve pide crossways; slice through each half horizontally. Shred half of the basil.

Place pide pieces, cut side up, on unoiled oven tray. Spread sauce over pide; sprinkle with the shredded basil, chicken, fetta and combined grated cheeses. Bake in moderately hot oven about 15 minutes or until cheeses melt and brown lightly. Serve sprinkled with remaining basil.

pitta salad
sandwich

150g button mushrooms, sliced

1 medium (170g) red onion, sliced

1 small (150g) green capsicum, sliced thinly

3/4 cup (90g) seeded black olives, chopped

100g fetta cheese, crumbled

4 pitta pocket breads

1/3 cup (80ml) hummus

1 small red coral lettuce

lemon vinaigrette

1 teaspoon grated lemon rind

2 tablespoons lemon juice

1 clove garlic, crushed

1 tablespoon chopped fresh mint leaves

1/4 cup (60ml) olive oil

1 teaspoon Dijon mustard

Combine mushrooms, onion, capsicum, olives, cheese and Lemon Vinaigrette in bowl; mix well. Cut pocket breads in half; spread hummus inside, fill with lettuce and mushroom mixture.
Lemon Vinaigrette Combine all ingredients in jar; shake well.

nice 'n' spicy
wedges

5 large (1.5kg) potatoes

1 tablespoon cornflour

5 tablespoons ghee

1 medium (150g) onion, chopped finely

2 cloves garlic, crushed

2 teaspoons grated fresh ginger

1 teaspoon brown mustard seeds

1 teaspoon cumin seeds

2 teaspoons garam masala

$1/2$ teaspoon chilli powder

1 teaspoon salt

$1/4$ cup (60ml) lemon juice

2 tablespoons finely chopped fresh coriander leaves

Halve potatoes lengthways; cut each half into 3 wedges. Boil, steam or microwave potatoes until almost tender; drain. When cool, toss potatoes in cornflour.

Heat about 1 tablespoon of the ghee in medium pan; cook onion, garlic and ginger, stirring, until onion is soft. Add seeds, garam masala, chilli and salt; cook, stirring, until fragrant.

Heat half the remaining ghee in large pan; cook half the potatoes about 5 minutes or until browned and crisp all sides. Remove from pan, keep warm; repeat with remaining ghee and potatoes.

Toss potatoes in same pan with spice mixture, juice and coriander.

12 quick 'n' easy
artichoke pizzas

2 tablespoons light olive oil

3 medium (450g) onions, sliced

2 x 26cm or 4 x 12cm packaged pizza bases

$2/3$ cup (160ml) tomato paste

$1/2$ cup (60g) grated cheddar cheese

$1/2$ cup (100g) sun-dried capsicums in oil, drained, sliced

10 canned artichoke hearts, drained, quartered

$1/3$ cup (40g) seeded black olives, quartered

$11/2$ cups (185g) grated cheddar cheese, extra

$1/3$ cup (25g) grated parmesan cheese

$1/4$ cup basil leaves

Heat oil in medium pan, add onion; cook, stirring, until soft, drain on absorbent paper. Spread pizza bases with tomato paste; top with cheddar cheese, onion, capsicum, artichokes, olives, extra cheddar and parmesan cheese.
Place pizzas on oven tray; bake in moderately hot oven about 15 minutes or until lightly browned. Serve topped with basil.

speedy
minestrone

30g butter

1 medium (150g)
onion, thinly sliced

1 clove garlic, crushed

2 bacon rashers,
chopped

1 stick celery, chopped

1 medium (120g)
carrot, chopped

425g can tomatoes

310g can red kidney
beans, drained

3 cups (750ml) water

1 small chicken stock
cube, crumbled

$1/3$ cup (60g) short
pasta

$1/4$ cup (20g) grated
fresh parmesan
cheese

Heat butter in large pan; add onion, garlic and bacon, stir over medium
heat about 2 minutes or until onion is soft. Add celery and carrot to pan;
stir over heat further 2 minutes. Stir in undrained crushed tomatoes,
beans, water, stock cube and pasta. Bring to boil, reduce heat, cover;
simmer 30 minutes. Serve topped with cheese.

14 polenta pizza with
marinated beef

400g piece beef rump steak

$^1/_4$ cup (60ml) lemon juice

2 cloves garlic, crushed

1 teaspoon seasoned pepper

1 cup (150g) self-raising flour

$^1/_2$ cup (80g) wholemeal self-raising flour

$^1/_4$ cup (40g) polenta

20g butter

$^1/_2$ cup (125ml) water, approximately

$^1/_3$ cup (80ml) tomato paste

1$^1/_2$ cups (150g) grated mozzarella cheese

2 tablespoons shredded fresh basil leaves

$^1/_2$ cup (40g) shaved parmesan cheese

onion topping

2 tablespoons water

1 clove garlic, crushed

2 medium (300g) onions, sliced

1 medium (200g) red capsicum, sliced

Combine beef, juice, garlic and pepper in bowl; mix well. Cover; refrigerate 15 minutes.

Sift flours into large bowl; stir in polenta, rub in butter. Add enough water to mix to a soft dough. Knead dough on floured surface until smooth. Roll dough until large enough to fit oiled 31cm pizza pan; lift into pan, pinch edge.

Spread paste over dough; sprinkle with one-third of the mozzarella cheese, top with Onion Topping then remaining mozzarella. Bake pizza in moderately hot oven about 25 minutes or until well browned.

Meanwhile, drain beef from marinade; discard marinade. Add beef to heated large non-stick pan; cook until browned both sides and cooked as desired. Slice beef thinly. Top cooked pizza with sliced beef, basil and parmesan cheese; serve immediately.

Onion Topping Combine all ingredients in pan; cook, stirring, over low heat, until onions are soft and liquid has evaporated.

16 tomato, fetta and spinach
galettes

250g frozen spinach, thawed

2 sheets ready-rolled puff pastry

1/3 cup (80ml) bottled pesto sauce with sun-dried tomatoes

200g fetta cheese, crumbled

1/4 cup finely chopped fresh basil leaves

250g cherry tomatoes, halved

1/4 cup (20g) coarsely grated parmesan cheese

1 teaspoon cracked black pepper

Drain spinach; using hands, squeeze excess liquid from spinach, chop spinach roughly.

Oil 2 oven trays; place 1 sheet of pastry on each. Fold edges of pastry in to form 1cm border; pinch corners of bases together. Divide pesto between bases; spread evenly to cover base. Top each with spinach, fetta, basil and tomatoes; sprinkle with parmesan cheese and pepper.

Bake in hot oven about 15 minutes or until crisp and browned lightly.

mexican pizza

26cm packaged pizza base

1 tablespoon taco seasoning mix

450g can refried beans

150g sliced rare roast beef, halved

1 cup (100g) grated mozzarella cheese

1 small (200g) avocado, mashed

1 teaspoon lemon juice

1 medium (190g) tomato, chopped finely

1/2 small (50g) red onion, chopped finely

1 tablespoon chopped fresh flat-leaf parsley

1/4 cup (60ml) sour cream

Place pizza base on oven tray; spread with combined seasoning mix and beans. Top with beef and cheese. Bake in moderately hot oven about 15 minutes or until browned lightly. **Meanwhile**, combine avocado and juice in small bowl. Combine tomato, onion and parsley in small bowl. Serve pizza topped with avocado mixture, tomato mixture and sour cream.

18 pocket

pizzas

200g minced beef
4 pitta pocket breads
1/3 cup (80ml) tomato paste
130g can corn kernels, drained
1/2 medium (100g) red
capsicum, sliced
1/2 small (40g) onion, sliced
4 cherry tomatoes, sliced
1 cup (125g) grated cheddar
cheese

Add beef to heated non-stick medium pan; cook, stirring, until well browned. Place pocket breads on oven tray, spread with tomato paste. Top pocket breads with beef, corn, capsicum, onion and tomatoes; sprinkle with cheese.
Bake in moderately hot oven about 15 minutes or until browned lightly.

savoury mince and
cabbage-topped potatoes

4 large (1.2kg)
potatoes

1 tablespoon
vegetable oil

500g minced beef

1 medium (150g)
onion, chopped

$1/4$ cup (60ml) tomato
paste

$1/2$ x 40g packet
chicken noodle soup

$1^1/2$ cups (375ml)
water

2 teaspoons
Worcestershire sauce

1 medium (200g) red
capsicum, chopped

$1/2$ medium (750g)
Chinese cabbage,
chopped finely

2 tablespoons
chopped fresh parsley

Wash and dry potatoes. Place potatoes on oven tray; bake in moderately
hot oven about 1 hour or until soft.

Meanwhile, heat oil in large pan, add beef, cook, stirring, until browned.
Add onion to same pan; cook, stirring, until onion is soft. Add paste, dry
soup mix, water, sauce and capsicum to pan; simmer, covered, about
30 minutes or until thickened. Stir in cabbage.

Cut cross in top of each potato, pinch to open slightly. Spoon beef
mixture over potatoes, sprinkle with parsley.

20 roasted capsicum and fetta muffins

1 medium (200g) red capsicum

1 medium (200g) yellow capsicum

2¹/₂ cups (375g) self-raising flour

100g fetta cheese, chopped

¹/₂ cup (40g) grated parmesan cheese

90g butter, melted

1 egg, lightly beaten

1 cup (250ml) milk

1 tablespoon chopped fresh rosemary

¹/₂ teaspoon ground black pepper

1 tablespoon sesame seeds

Grease 6-hole Texas (³/₄ cup/180ml) muffin pan.

Quarter capsicums, remove seeds and membranes. Roast under grill or in very hot oven, skin-side up, until skin blisters and blackens. Cover capsicum pieces in plastic or paper for 5 minutes, remove skin. Roughly chop capsicums.

Sift flour into large bowl; stir in capsicum, cheeses, butter, egg, milk, rosemary and pepper. Divide mixture among holes of prepared pan, sprinkle with seeds.

Bake in moderately hot oven about 30 minutes.

22 eggplant and
butter **bean** pizzas

300g can butter beans

165g jar pesto sauce with roasted capsicum

¹/₄ cup (20g) grated parmesan cheese

3 (180g) baby eggplants

1 long loaf Turkish pide

6 green onions, sliced thinly

Blend or process undrained butter beans, 2 teaspoons of the pesto and the cheese until smooth. Using a vegetable peeler, peel strips from eggplants. Cut pide crossways into 4 pieces; split each piece in half, place pide pieces, cut-side up on oven tray.

Spread remaining pesto then bean mixture over pide; top with eggplant and all but 2 tablespoons of the onion. Bake in moderately hot oven about 15 minutes or until browned and crisp. Serve sprinkled with remaining onion and extra shaved parmesan, if desired.

bacon and garlic tomato
soup

1 tablespoon oil

1 large (200g) onion, chopped

3 cloves garlic, crushed

1 teaspoon grated fresh ginger

3 bacon rashers, chopped

$1/2$ teaspoon chilli powder

2 x 425g cans tomatoes

1 tablespoon tomato paste

1 small chicken stock cube, crumbled

1 cup (250ml) water

$1/3$ cup (80ml) dry red wine

Heat oil in large saucepan, add onion, garlic, ginger and bacon; stir over medium heat about 3 minutes or until bacon is cooked. Stir in chilli, undrained crushed tomatoes, paste, stock cube, water and wine.
Bring to boil, reduce heat; simmer, uncovered, 5 minutes. Blend or process mixture, in batches, until well combined. Return to pan; reheat before serving.

toasted prawn
sandwiches

8 slices bread

butter

250g cooked shelled prawns, chopped finely

$1/4$ cup (60ml) mayonnaise

1 cup (125g) grated cheddar cheese

2 green onions, chopped

$1/2$ teaspoon dry mustard

1 tablespoon tomato paste

2 teaspoons chopped fresh dill

few drops Tabasco sauce

Spread bread with butter on 1 side. Combine remaining ingredients in medium bowl; spoon over unbuttered side of half the bread slices.

Top with remaining bread slices, buttered-side up. Place sandwiches in jaffle iron or sandwich maker; cook until browned both sides and heated through.

seafood

and bacon pizza

4 bacon rashers,
chopped

$1/4$ cup (60ml) tomato
pasta sauce

1 medium (150g)
onion, chopped finely

$1/2$ x 500g packet
frozen cooked mussel
meat, thawed, drained,
chopped

375g uncooked
medium prawns,
shelled, chopped

1 medium (200g)
green capsicum,
chopped

2 cups (200g) grated
mozzarella cheese

$1/2$ teaspoon dried
oregano leaves

scone dough

1 cup (150g) self-
raising flour

15g butter

$1/3$ cup (80ml) milk,
approximately

Cook bacon in medium pan until crisp; drain on
absorbent paper.

Roll Scone Dough on floured surface until large
enough to fit oiled 31cm pizza pan; lift dough
into pan.

Spread dough with sauce; top with onion,
chopped mussel meat, prawns, capsicum,
bacon, cheese and oregano. Bake in hot oven
15 minutes or until browned lightly.

Scone Dough Sift flour into bowl, rub in butter,
add enough milk to mix to a firm dough. Knead
dough on floured surface until smooth.

spicy beef pizza

2 teaspoons olive oil

250g minced beef

1 small (80g) onion, sliced thinly

1 clove garlic, crushed

1 teaspoon ground cumin

1/2 teaspoon ground coriander

1/2 teaspoon sweet paprika

pinch ground cinnamon

1 small (70g) carrot, grated

1 small (90g) zucchini, grated

1/2 x 400g can tomatoes

2 tablespoons tomato paste

1 tablespoon chopped fresh coriander leaves

26cm packaged pizza base

1 tablespoon pine nuts, toasted

yogurt topping

1/2 cup (125ml) yogurt

1 tablespoon chopped fresh coriander leaves

1/2 teaspoon ground cumin

1 teaspoon honey

1 teaspoon lemon juice

Heat oil in medium pan, add beef; cook, stirring, until browned. Add onion, garlic and spices; cook, stirring, until onion is soft. Stir in carrot, zucchini, undrained crushed tomatoes, paste and coriander. Simmer, covered, until thick, stirring occasionally; cool slightly.

Place pizza base on oven tray, top with beef mixture. Bake in moderately hot oven about 15 minutes or until browned. Top pizza with Yogurt Topping, sprinkle with pine nuts and extra coriander, if desired.

Yogurt Topping Combine all ingredients in bowl; mix well.

omelette

8 eggs, beaten lightly

1/2 cup (125ml) milk

1/2 teaspoon ground black pepper

30g butter

2 medium (380g) tomatoes, sliced

2 slices ham, chopped

125g packet cheese spread with chives, sliced

Combine eggs, milk and pepper in bowl; mix well. Heat butter in large pan; pour in egg mixture, cook 2 minutes. Place tomatoes and ham on one side of omelette; cook until underside of omelette is set.

Top tomatoes and ham with cheese, fold omelette over filling· cook until omelette is set and cheese just melted. Cut into wedges to serve.

satay

chicken pizza

Pizza cheese is a shredded blend of processed mozzarella, cheddar and parmesan cheeses.

26cm packaged pizza base

1 cup (125g) pizza cheese

2 cups (340g) chopped cooked chicken

1/3 cup (80ml) bottled satay sauce

1 tablespoon vegetable oil

1 small (70g) carrot

1/2 cup (40g) bean sprouts

1 green onion, sliced

1 tablespoon unsalted roasted peanuts, chopped

2 teaspoons chopped fresh coriander leaves

Place pizza base on oven tray; sprinkle with cheese.

Combine chicken with sauce in large bowl; spoon over cheese, drizzle with oil. Bake in moderately hot oven 15 minutes or until topping is hot.

Meanwhile, cut carrot into long thin strips. Top pizza with carrot and remaining ingredients.

fried salmon
sandwiches

210g can red salmon, drained

1 clove garlic, crushed

1/2 small (75g) red capsicum, chopped finely

3 green onions, chopped finely

1/2 cup (60g) grated cheddar cheese

1 tablespoon mayonnaise

8 slices white bread

1 egg, lightly beaten

2 tablespoons milk

vegetable oil, for shallow-frying

Combine salmon, garlic, capsicum, onion, cheese and mayonnaise in medium bowl; mix well.

Flatten bread slightly, using a rolling pin. Cut 8 rounds from bread with a 9cm cutter. Spread salmon mixture on 4 of the bread rounds; top with remaining bread rounds, press together firmly. Dip sandwiches into combined egg and milk. Heat oil in pan; shallow-fry sandwiches until browned both sides, drain on absorbent paper.

tomato, eggplant and
peperoni pizza

1 medium (300g)
eggplant

coarse cooking salt

$1/3$ cup (80m) olive oil

26cm packaged pizza
base

2 cloves garlic,
crushed

3 small (390g)
tomatoes, sliced

100g peperoni, sliced

$1/2$ cup (100g) ricotta
cheese

1 tablespoon pine nuts

$1^1/2$ tablespoons
shredded fresh
basil leaves

Thinly slice eggplant, place in colander, sprinkle with salt; stand
20 minutes. Rinse eggplant slices under cold water, drain, pat dry with
absorbent paper. Brush eggplant slices with $1/4$ cup (60ml) of the olive oil;
grill until lightly browned both sides.

Place pizza base on oven tray; brush with half the remaining oil and
garlic. Overlap tomato and eggplant slices on pizza, top with peperoni,
cheese, nuts, remaining oil and basil. Bake in moderately hot oven about
15 minutes or until browned.

32 dips for wedges

Cut 4 large (1.2kg) potatoes into thin wedges. Place on oven trays; drizzle with 1 tablespoon olive oil, sprinkle with salt and pepper to taste. Cook, uncovered, in very hot oven about 30 minutes or until browned.

avocado, sour cream and chilli dip

Blend or process 1 medium (250g) avocado with 1/2 cup (125ml) sour cream and 1 tablespoon lime juice until smooth. Stir in 2 tablespoons sweet chilli sauce, 1/2 small (50g) red onion, finely chopped, and 1 small (130g) tomato, seeded and chopped finely.

warm cheese and olive dip

Combine 250g package light cream cheese with 1/2 cup (60g) grated cheddar cheese, 1/4 cup (40g) seeded chopped green olives, 1 clove crushed garlic and 1/2 cup (125ml) milk in medium pan; stir over low heat until ingredients are heated through. Stir in 1 tablespoon finely chopped fresh basil leaves.

roasted red capsicum dip

Heat 1 tablespoon olive oil in small pan; add ¹/₂ medium (75g) chopped onion. Cook, stirring until soft. Quarter 3 medium (600g) capsicums; remove seeds and membranes. Roast under hot grill or in very hot oven, skin-side up, until skin blisters and blackens. Wrap capsicum pieces in plastic or paper for 5 minutes, peel away skin; chop roughly. Blend or process capsicum with onion mixture and 1 tablespoon balsamic vinegar until smooth. Season with salt and pepper to taste.

from left: avocado, sour cream and
chilli dip; warm cheese and olive dip;
roasted red capsicum dip;
caramelised chilli and onion dip

caramelised chilli and onion dip

Melt 50g butter in medium pan; cook 2 large (600g) sliced red onions and 1 clove crushed garlic, stirring, until soft and browned lightly. Add 2 tablespoons brown sugar, 1 tablespoon balsamic vinegar, 2 tablespoons chicken stock and 2 tablespoons sweet chilli sauce; cook, stirring, until onions are caramelised.

spicy sausage and corn
muffins

1³/₄ cups (260g) self-raising flour

1 teaspoon dried crushed chilli

¹/₂ teaspoon ground cumin

¹/₂ teaspoon ground coriander

1 teaspoon hot paprika

³/₄ cup (90g) coarsely grated smoked cheese

90g chorizo sausage, chopped

¹/₂ medium (100g) red capsicum, chopped

¹/₂ medium (100g) green capsicum, chopped

1 clove garlic, crushed

1 small (80g) onion, grated

130g can creamed corn

2 eggs, beaten lightly

90g butter, melted

1 cup (250ml) buttermilk

¹/₂ teaspoon hot paprika, extra

Grease 6-hole Texas (³/₄ cup/180ml) muffin pan.
Sift flour into large bowl, add chilli, spices,
cheese, sausage and capsicum; mix well. Add
garlic, onion and corn then stir in eggs, butter
and buttermilk. Spoon mixture into prepared
pan; sprinkle with extra paprika. Bake in
moderately hot oven about 25 minutes.

Makes 6

pesto pizzas with

ricotta and capsicums

Quarter capsicums, remove seeds and membranes. Roast under grill or in very hot oven, skin-side up, until skin blisters and blackens. Cover capsicum pieces in plastic or paper for 5 minutes, peel away skin. Cut capsicums into strips.

Spread Pesto over pitta breads; spread with ricotta cheese, top with capsicum strips. Place pizzas on oven tray, bake in moderately hot oven about 15 minutes or until heated through and crisp.

Pesto Blend or process almonds, basil, garlic, parmesan cheese and sugar until smooth. Add oil gradually, in a thin stream while motor is operating, until oil has been absorbed and mixture is smooth.

1 medium (200g) red capsicum

1 medium (200g) green capsicum

4 small pitta breads

1 cup (200g) ricotta cheese

pesto

$^1/_4$ cup (40g) blanched almonds, toasted

1 cup firmly packed fresh basil leaves

1 clove garlic, crushed

2 tablespoons grated parmesan cheese

1 teaspoon sugar

$^1/_3$ cup (80ml) olive oil

crispy bake

2¹/₂ cups (425g) chopped cooked chicken

3 sticks celery, sliced

³/₄ cup (105g) slivered almonds

1¹/₂ cups (375ml) mayonnaise

¹/₂ cup (125ml) cream

1 small (80g) onion, chopped finely

1 tablespoon lemon juice

1 cup (125g) grated cheddar cheese

50g packet potato chips, crushed

Combine chicken, celery, almonds, mayonnaise, cream, onion and juice in large bowl; spoon into shallow heatproof dish. Sprinkle with combined cheese and chips; bake in moderate oven about 20 minutes or until browned and crisp.

38 satay lamb

pizza

2 teaspoons olive oil

350g lamb fillets, sliced thinly

26cm packaged pizza base

$1/4$ cup (60ml) sweet chilli sauce

$1/4$ cup chopped fresh coriander leaves

1 medium (150g) onion, sliced

1 small (150g) red capsicum, sliced

1 medium (200g) yellow capsicum, sliced

$1/3$ cup (80ml) bottled satay sauce

Heat oil in large shallow pan, add lamb; cook, stirring, until browned. Place pizza base on oven tray; spread with combined chilli sauce and coriander. Top with onion, capsicum and lamb. Drizzle with satay sauce. Bake in moderately hot oven about 15 minutes or until base is crisp.

crisp pitta
triangles

250g packet cream cheese, softened

2 teaspoons ground cumin

2 green onions, chopped

12 slices mild salami, chopped finely

2 cloves garlic, crushed

4 small pitta pocket breads

90g butter

Beat cheese, cumin, onions, salami and garlic in small bowl with electric mixer until combined. **Split** each pocket bread in half, spread salami mixture onto 4 halves; sandwich together with remaining halves. Spread butter onto both sides of pocket breads; cook in heated pan until lightly browned each side and crisp, drain on absorbent paper. To serve, cut each pocket bread into 8 triangles.

soup

250g boneless white fish fillets, chopped

3 cups (750ml) water

410ml can coconut milk

1 onion, chopped

1 tablespoon grated fresh ginger

2 tablespoons chopped fresh lemon grass

1 small fresh red chilli, chopped

1 tablespoon fish sauce

2 tablespoons lime juice

100g Chinese cabbage, shredded

$^1/_4$ cup chopped fresh coriander leaves

Combine all ingredients in large pan, bring to boil; simmer, uncovered, 10 minutes or until fish is tender. Serve immediately.

peperoni
pizzas

26cm packaged pizza base

1/2 cup (125ml) tomato pasta sauce

1 tablespoon chopped fresh basil leaves

1 teaspoon chopped fresh thyme

1/2 cup (60g) grated cheddar cheese

80g button mushrooms, sliced

1 small (150g) red capsicum, sliced

1 small (150g) green capsicum, sliced

50g sliced peperoni

1 cup (125g) grated cheddar cheese, extra

Place pizza base on oven tray; spread with combined sauce and herbs, top with cheese, mushrooms, capsicum and peperoni. Sprinkle with extra cheese. Bake in moderately hot oven about 15 minutes or until browned.

350g lamb fillets

2 cloves garlic, crushed

2 small fresh red chillies, seeded, chopped finely

1 tablespoon lemon juice

2 teaspoons cracked black pepper

2 teaspoons chopped fresh thyme

30g butter

1 tablespoon olive oil

1 large (300g) red onion, sliced thinly

2 tablespoons brown sugar

1 tablespoon balsamic vinegar

1 medium (200g) red capsicum

1 medium (200g) yellow capsicum

1 long loaf Turkish pide

2/3 cup (160ml) hot relish

2 small fresh red chillies, seeded, chopped finely, extra

2 1/2 cups (250g) grated mozzarella cheese

1/2 cup (40g) grated parmesan cheese

Cut lamb into 1.5cm slices. Combine lamb with garlic, chilli, juice, pepper and half the thyme in large bowl; mix well. Cover; refrigerate 10 minutes.

Heat butter and oil in small pan, add onion, cook, stirring, until onion is very soft. Add sugar and vinegar to same pan, cook, stirring, until mixture is thick and syrupy.

Quarter capsicums, remove seeds and membranes. Roast under grill or in very hot oven, skin-side up, until skin blisters and blackens. Cover capsicum pieces in plastic or paper for 5 minutes, peel away skin. Cut capsicums into 1cm slices.

Halve pide crossways; place, split-side up, on greased oven trays; spread with combined relish and extra chilli, top with onion mixture, lamb mixture, then mozzarella cheese. Top with strips of capsicum, sprinkle with parmesan cheese and remaining thyme. Bake in moderately hot oven 15 minutes or until pizzas are browned and lamb is cooked through.

44 pumpkin and leek soup

40g butter

1 large (500g) leek, sliced

1kg butternut pumpkin, chopped

2 medium (400g) potatoes, chopped

4 cups (1 litre) chicken stock

1/2 cup (125ml) milk

1/2 cup (125ml) cream

Heat butter in large pan; cook leek, stirring, until soft.

Meanwhile, boil, steam or microwave pumpkin and potato, separately, until tender; drain. Mash pumpkin and potato together; add to pan with leek mixture. Stir in stock and milk.

Blend or process mixture, in batches, until smooth. Return mixture to clean pan; stir over heat until heated through. Ladle soup into serving bowls; swirl cream into soup.

cheesy tuna

pizza

26cm packaged pizza base

³/₄ cup (180ml) chunky vegetable pasta sauce

2 small (180g) zucchini, sliced

200g large flat mushrooms, chopped

180g can tuna in brine, drained

2 teaspoons lemon juice

1 cup (125g) grated cheddar cheese

¹/₂ teaspoon chopped fresh dill

1 teaspoon chopped fresh chives

Spread pizza base with sauce; top with zucchini, mushrooms, combined tuna and juice, cheese and herbs. Place pizza on oven tray; bake in moderately hot oven about 15 minutes or until top is browned.

*1¹/₂ cups (225g)
self-raising flour*

30g butter

*¹/₂ cup (125ml) milk,
approximately*

*60g button mushrooms,
sliced*

*¹/₂ medium (100g) green
capsicum, chopped finely*

*¹/₂ medium (100g) red
capsicum, chopped finely*

*1¹/₂ cups (185g) grated
cheddar cheese*

*¹/₂ teaspoon sweet
paprika*

mince topping

1 tablespoon olive oil

*1 small (80g) onion,
chopped finely*

1 clove garlic, crushed

250g minced beef

400g can tomatoes

*2 tablespoons tomato
paste*

¹/₂ small beef stock cube

¹/₂ teaspoon sugar

*¹/₄ teaspoon dried
oregano leaves*

frypan pizza

Sift flour into large bowl; rub in butter, add enough milk to mix to a soft dough. Knead dough on lightly floured surface until smooth.

Press dough evenly into 23cm frying pan; spread with Mince Topping, sprinkle with mushrooms, capsicum and cheese.

Cover pan, cook over medium heat about 20 minutes or until pizza is browned underneath and cooked through. Sprinkle with paprika.

Mince Topping Heat oil in pan, add onion and garlic; cook, stirring, until onion is soft. Add beef, cook, stirring, until beef is browned. Add undrained crushed tomatoes and remaining ingredients; simmer, uncovered, until thick, cool.

48 pesto salami
muffins

2 cups (300g) self-raising flour

1¹/₂ cups (210g) chopped mild salami

¹/₃ cup (80ml) bottled pesto

3 eggs, beaten lightly

¹/₃ cup (80ml) vegetable oil

¹/₂ cup (125ml) buttermilk

²/₃ cup (80g) grated gruyere cheese

pesto cream

¹/₂ cup (125ml) sour cream

2 tablespoons bottled pesto

Grease 12-hole (¹/₃ cup/80ml) muffin pan.

Sift flour into large bowl; stir in salami, pesto, eggs, oil and buttermilk. Spoon mixture into prepared pan, sprinkle with cheese. Bake in moderately hot oven about 20 minutes. Serve with Pesto Cream.

Pesto Cream Combine ingredients in a bowl; mix well.

Makes 12

salami

pizza

Sift flour into large bowl; rub in butter, add enough milk to mix to a soft dough. Knead dough on floured surface until smooth. Roll dough until large enough to line oiled 31cm pizza pan; lift dough into pan. **Spread** dough with paste; top with tomato, onion, salami, capsicum and mushrooms; sprinkle with herbs and cheese. Bake in hot oven 20 minutes or until lightly browned.

2 cups (300g) self-raising flour

40g butter

³/₄ cup (180ml) milk, approximately

¹/₃ cup (80ml) tomato paste

1 medium (190g) tomato, sliced

1 medium (150g) onion, sliced

60g sliced mild salami

1 small (150g) green capsicum, sliced

60g button mushrooms, sliced

1 teaspoon dried basil leaves

¹/₂ teaspoon dried oregano

1 cup (100g) grated mozzarella cheese

50 chicken and
crunchy noodle pizza

1 tablespoon vegetable oil

4 (500g) chicken thigh fillets

26cm packaged pizza base

100g fried noodles, crushed lightly

1 cup (100g) coarsely grated mozzarella cheese

1/4 cup (60ml) sweet chilli sauce

1 tablespoon soy sauce

pesto

1 cup firmly packed fresh basil leaves

1 tablespoon (40g) slivered almonds, toasted, chopped

1 clove garlic, crushed

2 tablespoons olive oil

Heat oil in large pan; cook chicken, until browned both sides and cooked through. Drain chicken on absorbent paper; cut into 5mm slices.

Spread Pesto evenly over pizza base; top with chicken. Sprinkle combined noodles and cheese over chicken; drizzle with combined sauces. Place pizza on oven tray; bake in moderate oven about 20 minutes or until lightly browned.

Pesto Blend or process all ingredients until smooth and thick.

bolognese
jaffles

1 tablespoon olive oil

1 medium (150g)
onion, chopped

1 clove garlic, crushed

250g minced beef

$1/2$ x 400g can
tomatoes

2 tablespoons tomato
paste

1 beef stock cube

$1/2$ teaspoon sugar

1 tablespoon chopped
fresh basil leaves

12 slices white bread

butter

Heat oil in medium pan, add onion, garlic and beef; cook, stirring, until
beef is well browned. Add undrained crushed tomatoes, paste, crumbled
stock cube and sugar to pan; simmer, uncovered, about 10 minutes or
until mixture is thick. Stir in basil.

Spread bread with butter on one side; spoon beef mixture onto
unbuttered side of half the bread slices. Top with remaining bread slices,
buttered-side up. Place sandwiches in jaffle iron or sandwich maker; cook
until browned both sides and heated through.

Makes 6

52 polenta-base
pizza

3¹/₂ cups (875ml) water

1 cup (170g) polenta

¹/₂ cup (40g) grated parmesan cheese

¹/₃ cup (80ml) tomato paste

2 cups (200g) grated mozzarella cheese

¹/₂ cup (40g) grated parmesan cheese, extra

topping

2 tablespoons olive oil

2 medium (300g) onions, sliced

2 cloves garlic, crushed

¹/₄ cup (40g) pine nuts

1 medium (200g) red capsicum, sliced

¹/₂ cup (80g) black olives

¹/₄ cup shredded fresh basil leaves

Bring water to boil in large pan; add polenta, simmer 10 minutes, stirring occasionally, until polenta is very thick. Stir in ¹/₂ cup parmesan cheese. Spread mixture onto oiled 31cm pizza pan; refrigerate 15 minutes. Spread paste over polenta; top with half the combined mozzarella and extra parmesan cheese.

Arrange Topping over cheese, sprinkle with remaining cheeses. Bake in moderately hot oven 20 minutes or until browned.

Topping Heat oil in pan, add onion, garlic and pine nuts; cook, stirring, until onion is soft. Add capsicum; cook, stirring, until softened. Stir in olives and basil.

54 jumbo chicken and
rocket sandwiches

1 small (70g) carrot

1 (130g) Lebanese cucumber

8 slices rye bread

60g rocket

1 small (100g) red onion, sliced

2 cups (340g) chopped cooked chicken

$1/3$ cup (80ml) mayonnaise

1 tablespoon seeded mustard

$1/2$ cup (100g) sun-dried capsicums in oil, drained, sliced

Using vegetable peeler, peel long thin strips from carrot and cucumber.

Top 4 bread slices with rocket, onion, chicken, combined mayonnaise and mustard, capsicum, carrot and cucumber.

Top with remaining bread slices.

covered pizzas

150g button mushrooms, sliced

75g sliced mild salami, chopped

1 small (150g) green capsicum, chopped

1 medium (190g) tomato, chopped

6 seeded black olives, chopped

2 cups (200g) grated mozzarella cheese

4 small pitta bread rounds

$1/3$ cup (80ml) tomato paste

$1/2$ cup (60g) grated cheddar cheese

$1/2$ teaspoon dried oregano

Combine mushrooms, salami, capsicum, tomato, olives and mozzarella cheese in medium bowl. Cut a slit down side of each pitta bread to form a pocket. Spread inside pockets with tomato paste; fill with mushroom mixture. Place pitta breads on oven trays; sprinkle with cheddar cheese and oregano. **Bake** in moderately hot oven about 15 minutes or until heated through and cheese is melted.

56 spring vegetable

soup

2 tablespoons vegetable oil

1 large (200g) onion, chopped

2 cloves garlic, crushed

1 medium (350g) leek, sliced

2 medium (240g) carrots, sliced

2 (150g) celery sticks, sliced

200g button mushrooms, chopped

1.25 litres (5 cups) vegetable stock

50g spaghettini (or any fine pasta)

1 tablespoon finely chopped fresh parsley

Heat oil in large pan; cook onion and garlic, stirring, until onion is soft. Add leek, carrot and celery; cook, stirring, until vegetables are soft. Add mushrooms; cook, stirring, 1 minute. Add stock to pan. Bring to boil; simmer, uncovered, 15 minutes.
Add pasta; cook, uncovered, until just tender. Stir parsley into soup.

asparagus

pesto pizza

500g asparagus

4 small pitta bread rounds

1 large (350g) red capsicum, chopped

500g mozzarella cheese, sliced

$^1/_2$ cup (40g) grated parmesan cheese

pesto

$^1/_3$ cup (80ml) light olive oil

2 tablespoons pine nuts, toasted

2 cups firmly packed fresh basil leaves

2 cloves garlic, chopped

$^1/_3$ cup (25g) grated parmesan cheese

Boil, steam or microwave asparagus until just tender; drain. Rinse under cold water; drain. Spread pitta breads with Pesto, top with asparagus, capsicum and both cheeses. Place pizzas on oven trays; bake in moderately hot oven about 15 minutes or until browned lightly.
Pesto Process all ingredients until smooth.

spinach and ham
frittata

2 tablespoons vegetable oil

1 medium (150g) onion, chopped

300g sliced ham, chopped

250g packet frozen spinach, thawed

1 medium (200g) red capsicum, chopped

6 eggs, beaten lightly

2 teaspoons seeded mustard

1 cup (125g) grated cheddar cheese

1/4 cup chopped fresh parsley

Heat oil in large non-stick frying pan, add onion and ham; cook, stirring, until onion is soft. Squeeze excess liquid from spinach, add to pan with capsicum; cook, stirring, until capsicum is soft. Pour combined eggs, mustard and half the cheese over mixture in pan; cook until well browned underneath. Sprinkle with remaining cheese, grill top of frittata until browned and set. Serve sprinkled with parsley.

glossary

bacon rashers also known as slices of bacon.

balsamic vinegar authentic only from the province of Modena, Italy; made from a regional wine of white Trebbiano grapes specially processed then aged in antique wooden casks to give the exquisite flavour.

bean sprouts also known as bean shoots.

beef, minced also known as ground beef.

butter use salted or unsalted "sweet" butter; 125g is equal to 1 stick of butter.

buttermilk low-fat milk cultured to give a slightly sour, tangy taste; low-fat yogurt can be substituted.

cabanossi a ready-to-eat sausage; also known as cabana.

cajun seasoning can include paprika, basil, onion, fennel, thyme, cayenne and tarragon.

capsicum also known as bell pepper.

cheese

cheddar: use an aged, full-flavoured variety.

cream: soft milk cheese commonly known as "Philadelphia" or "Philly".

fetta: Greek in origin; a crumbly textured goat or sheep milk cheese having a sharp, salty taste.

goat: made from goat milk, has an earthy, strong taste; comes in both soft and firm textures.

mozzarella: a semi-soft cheese with a delicate, fresh taste.

parmesan: a sharp-tasting, dry, hard cheese, made from skim or part-skim milk. We suggest you grate fresh parmesan cheese rather than use a pre-grated packaged variety.

ricotta: a sweet, fairly moist, fresh curd cheese having a low fat content.

chillies use rubber gloves when seeding and chopping fresh chillies as they can burn your skin; discard seeds to reduce the heat level.

dried crushed: available from supermarkets and Asian food stores.

powder: the Asian variety is the hottest, made from ground chillies.

sweet chilli sauce: a comparatively mild Thai-type commercial sauce made from red chillies, sugar, garlic and vinegar.

chorizo sausage spicy, made from pork, garlic and red peppers.

cornflour also known as cornstarch.

cream

fresh (minimum fat content 35%): also known as pure cream and pouring cream; has no additives.

sour (minimum fat content 35%): a thick, commercially cultured soured cream.

eggplant also known as aubergine.

flour

plain: an all-purpose flour, made from wheat.

self-raising: plain flour sifted with baking powder in the proportion of 1 cup flour to 2 teaspoons baking powder.

wholemeal self-raising: add baking powder to wholemeal plain flour as above to make wholemeal self-raising flour.

fried noodles crispy egg noodles packaged (commonly a 100g packet) already deep-fried.

garam masala a powdered blend of spices, based on varying proportions of cardamom, cinnamon, cloves, coriander and cumin. Sometimes chilli is added.

ghee clarified butter; with milk solids removed, this fat can be heated to a high temperature without burning. Used in Indian cooking.

ginger, fresh also known as green or root ginger; the thick gnarled root of a tropical plant.

herbs 1 teaspoon dried (not ground) is equal to 4 teaspoons chopped fresh herbs.

hummus a Middle-Eastern dip made of chickpeas, tahini (sesame paste), garlic and lemon juice.

milk we used full-cream homogenised milk unless otherwise specified.

mustard, seeded a coarse-grain; made of crushed

mustard seeds and Dijon-style mustard.

oil

olive, extra virgin: a high quality olive oil, obtained from the first pressing.

olive: a mono-unsaturated oil, made from the pressing of tree-ripened olives; especially good for everyday cooking and in salad dressings. Light describes the mild flavour, not the fat levels.

vegetable: any of a number of oils sourced from plant rather than animal fats.

onion

green: also known as scallion or (incorrectly) shallot; an immature onion picked before the bulb has formed, having a long, bright-green edible stalk.

red: also known as Spanish, red Spanish or Bermuda onion; a sweet-flavoured, large, purple-red onion that is particularly good raw.

spring: have crisp, narrow green-leafed tops and a fairly large sweet white bulb.

polenta a flour-like cereal made from ground corn (maize); similar to cornmeal but coarser and darker in colour; also the name given to the dish made from it.

prawns also known as shrimp.

refried beans pinto beans (similar to borlotti), cooked twice: soaked and boiled then mashed and fried, traditionally in lard. A Mexican staple, "frijoles refritos" or refried beans are available canned.

rocket a green salad leaf with a nutty taste.

soy sauce made from fermented soy beans. Several variations are available in most supermarkets and Asian food stores, among them are salt-reduced, light, sweet and salty.

spinach the green vegetable often called spinach is correctly known as Swiss chard, silverbeet or seakale.

stock cubes 1 crumbled stock cube is equivalent to 1 teaspoon of stock powder.

sugar the recipes in this book used coarse granulated table sugar, also known as crystal sugar, unless otherwise specified.

brown: a soft, fine granulated sugar containing molasses to give its characteristic colour.

tabasco sauce brand name of an extremely fiery sauce made from vinegar, hot red peppers and salt.

taco seasoning mix a packaged Mexican seasoning mix made from oregano, cumin, chillies and various other spices.

tomato

cherry: also known as Tiny Tim or Tom Thumb tomatoes, small and perfectly round.

paste: a concentrated tomato puree used to flavour soups, stews, sauces and casseroles.

puree: canned pureed tomatoes (not a concentrate). Use fresh, peeled, pureed tomatoes as a substitute.

sauce: also known as ketchup or catsup; a flavoured condiment based on tomatoes, vinegar and spices.

supreme: a canned product consisting of tomatoes, onions, celery, peppers, cheese and seasonings.

tandoori curry paste consisting of garlic, tamarind, ginger, coriander, chilli and spices.

tortillas thin, round unleavened bread originating in Mexico; can be made at home or purchased frozen, fresh or vacuum-packed. Two kinds are available, one made from wheat flour and the other from masa harina (maizemeal).

yogurt unflavoured, full-fat cow milk yogurt has been used in these recipes unless stated otherwise. Yogurt is also used to tenderise and thicken.

zucchini also known as courgette.

62 index

facts and figures 63

These conversions are approximate only, but the difference between an exact and the approximate conversion of various liquid and dry measures is minimal and will not affect your cooking results.

Note: NZ, Canada, USA and UK all use 15ml tablespoons. Australian tablespoons measure 20ml.
All cup and spoon measurements are level.

Measuring equipment
The difference between one country's measuring cups and another's is, at most, within a 2 or 3 teaspoon variance. (For the record, 1 Australian metric measuring cup holds approximately 250ml.) The most accurate way of measuring dry ingredients is to weigh them. For liquids, use a clear glass or plastic jug having metric markings.

How to measure
When using graduated measuring cups, shake dry ingredients loosely into the appropriate cup. Do not tap the cup on a bench or tightly pack the ingredients unless directed to do so. Level the top of measuring cups and measuring spoons with a knife. When measuring liquids, place a clear glass or plastic jug having metric markings on a flat surface to check accuracy at eye level.

Dry Measures

metric	imperial
15g	$1/2$oz
30g	1oz
60g	2oz
90g	3oz
125g	4oz ($1/4$lb)
155g	5oz
185g	6oz
220g	7oz
250g	8oz ($1/2$lb)
280g	9oz
315g	10oz
345g	11oz
375g	12oz ($3/4$lb)
410g	13oz
440g	14oz
470g	15oz
500g	16oz (1lb)
750g	24oz ($1 1/2$lb)
1kg	32oz (2lb)

We use large eggs having an average weight of 60g.

Liquid Measures

metric	imperial
30ml	1 fluid oz
60ml	2 fluid oz
100ml	3 fluid oz
125ml	4 fluid oz
150ml	5 fluid oz ($1/4$ pint/1 gill)
190ml	6 fluid oz
250ml (1cup)	8 fluid oz
300ml	10 fluid oz ($1/2$ pint)
500ml	16 fluid oz
600ml	20 fluid oz (1 pint)
1000ml (1litre)	$1 3/4$ pints

Helpful Measures

metric	imperial
3mm	$1/8$in
6mm	$1/4$in
1cm	$1/2$in
2cm	$3/4$in
2.5cm	1in
6cm	$2 1/2$in
8cm	3in
20cm	8in
23cm	9in
25cm	10in
30cm	12in (1ft)

Oven Temperatures
These oven temperatures are only a guide.
Always check the manufacturer's manual.

	°C (Celsius)	°F (Fahrenheit)	Gas Mark
Very slow	120	250	1
Slow	150	300	2
Moderately slow	160	325	3
Moderate	180 –190	350 – 375	4
Moderately hot	200 – 210	400 – 425	5
Hot	220 – 230	450 – 475	6
Very hot	240 – 250	500 – 525	7

Food editor Pamela Clark
Associate food editor Karen Hammial
Assistant food editor Kathy McGarry
Assistant recipe editor Elizabeth Hooper

HOME LIBRARY STAFF
Editor-in-chief Mary Coleman
Managing editor Susan Tomnay
Editor Julie Collard
Concept design Jackie Richards
Designer Jackie Richards
Book sales manager Jennifer McDonald
Group publisher Jill Baker
Publisher Sue Wannan
Chief executive officer John Alexander

Produced by *The Australian Women's Weekly*
Home Library, Sydney.

Colour separations by
ACP Colour Graphics Pty Ltd, Sydney.
Printing by Dai Nippon, Korea

Published by ACP Publishing Pty Limited,
54 Park St, Sydney; GPO Box 4088, Sydney,
NSW 1028. Ph: (02) 9282 8618
Fax: (02) 9267 9438.

awwhomelib@acp.com.au
www.awwbooks.com.au

Australia Distributed by Network Distribution
Company, GPO Box 4088, Sydney, NSW 1028.
Ph: (02) 9282 8777 Fax: (02) 9264 3278.

United Kingdom Distributed by Australian
Consolidated Press (UK), Moulton Park Business
Centre, Red House Rd, Moulton Park,
Northampton, NN3 6AQ. Ph: (01604) 497 531
Fax: (01604) 497 533 Acpukltd@aol.com

Canada Distributed by Whitecap Books Ltd,
351 Lynn Ave, North Vancouver, BC, V7J 2C4,
Ph: (604) 980 9852.

New Zealand Distributed by Netlink Distribution
Company, Level 4, 23 Hargreaves Street,
College Hill, Auckland 1, Ph: (9) 302 7616.

South Africa Distributed by PSD Promotions
(Pty) Ltd,PO Box 1175, Isando 1600, SA,
Ph: (011) 392 6065.
CNA Limited, Newsstand Division, PO Box 10799,
Johannesburg 2000. Ph: (011) 491 7500.

Make It Tonight: Pizzas and Snacks

Includes index.
ISBN 1 86396 097 X

1. Cookery, Italian.
I. Title: Australian Women's Weekly.
(Series: Australian Women's Weekly
make it tonight mini series).
641.5945

© ACP Publishing Pty Limited 1998
ABN 18 053 273 546

First published 1998. Reprinted 2001.

Cover: Quick and easy artichoke pizzas, page 12.
Stylist Vicki Liley
Photographer Scott Cameron
Board from Country Road
Back cover: Jumbo chicken and
rocket sandwiches, page 54.

mini books

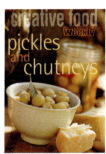

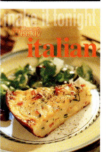

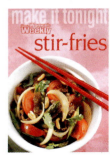